Las Vegas

Las Vegas

photographs by
santi visalli

foreword by
wayne newton

UNIVERSE

This page: A Joshua tree in Red Rock Canyon
Page 1: Detail of the Flamingo Hilton
Preceding overleaf: Retired neon sign at Young Electric Sign Co.

Published in the United States of America in 1996 by
Universe Publishing
A Division of Rizzoli International Publications, Inc.
300 Park Avenue South
New York, NY 10010

Library of Congress catalog number: 96-60683

Design by Jack* Design
Printed in Singapore

In memory of my father—a compulsive gambler

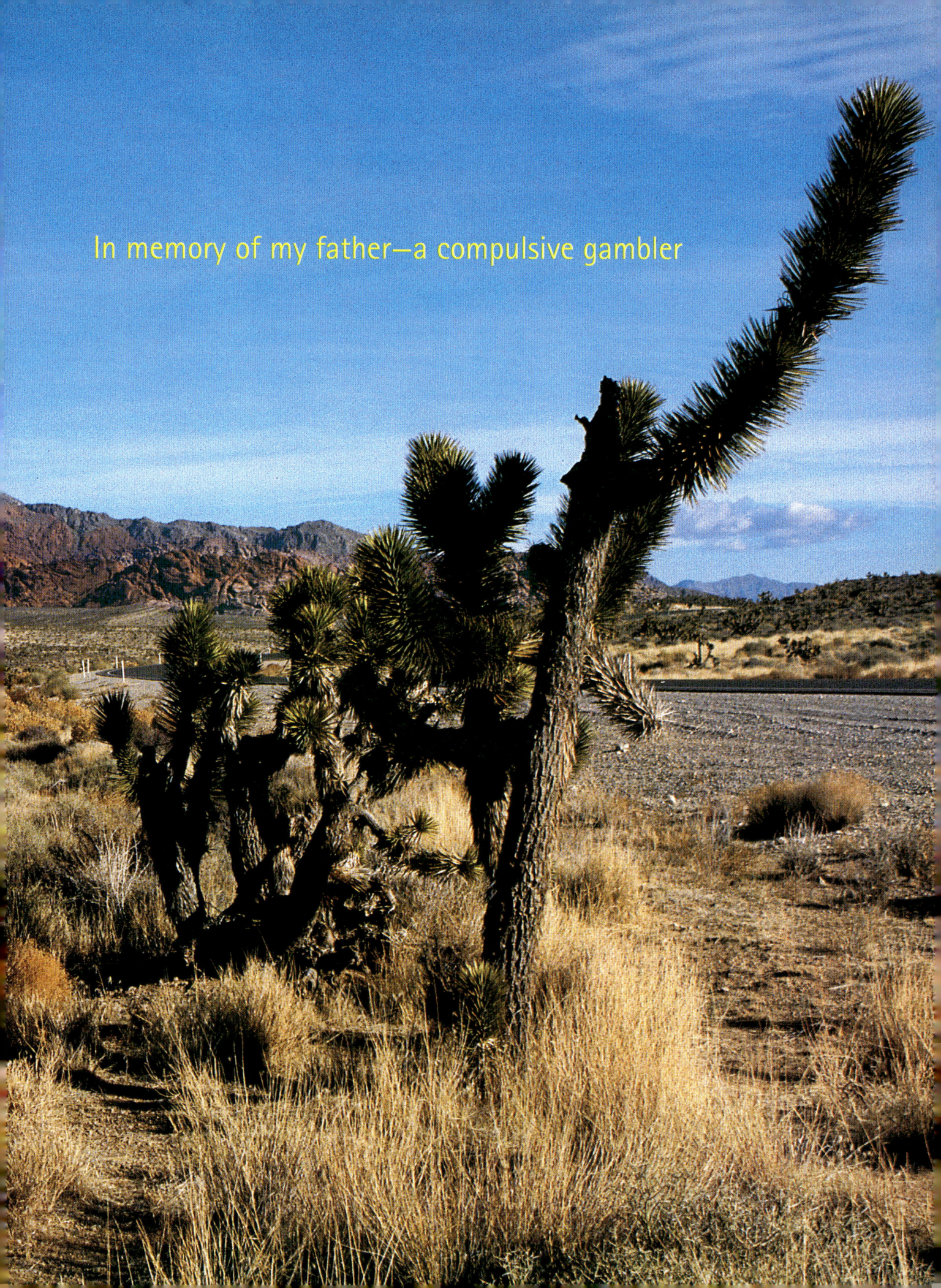

Wayne Newton

Las Vegas and I grew up and matured together in this past half-century. My brother Jerry and I were teenagers, working as a duo at the Fremont Hotel in the 1950s. We played in the lounge there six nights a week, six hours a night, forty-five minutes on and fifteen off. It was a tough grind but an incredible learning experience.

The late Bobby Darin saw us at the Copa Cabana and suggested changing the name from the Newton Brothers to Wayne Newton, which we did. He stayed on to give me my first hit record, "Danke Shoen"—a song intended as a follow-up to his own mega-hit, "Mack the Knife." Bobby actually produced the record and remained a good friend until his passing at much too young an age.

Jack Benny was the next great influence. My brother and I had decided we were ready to play a main show-room, and fortunately, Mr. Benny thought so too. He gave us our first main-room opportunity, up north at Harrah's, plus exposure on his national television show. Our lounge days were over.

During the 1950s, the Sands, the Desert Inn, Dunes, and the Riviera were just coming into existence, soon to be followed by Caesars Palace, the Landmark (now a convention center parking lot), and the International (now the Las Vegas Hilton). The Sands, home base for Sinatra and the Rat Pack, which included Dean Martin, Sammy Davis, Jr., Peter Lawford, Joey Bishop, and occasionally Danny Thomas, was responsible for one of the city's great growth periods—the 1950s and 1960s.

In the early 1970s, my brother Jerry decided that the business world was for him and we parted company. It took me a while to adjust. The wonderful Sands Copa Room became my personal bailiwick in the 1970s and 1980s. Working under the direction of Howard Hughes's closest personal friend, the late Walter Kane, I spent at least forty weeks a year, seven nights a week, two shows a night, dividing my time between Hughes's hotels—the Sands, the Frontier and the Desert Inn. I knew every board and nail in all three of those stages. Now, only the Desert Inn has showroom entertainment, the Sands is due to close in June, 1996, and the Frontier has been without shows for several years and has no apparent intention of resuming soon. Things never stop changing in this town.

But it hasn't always been this way. In the early 1800s, there was very little in this area. Next to nothing might be a better description. What was to become Las Vegas was an oasis, a water hole surrounded by a little greenery and a lot of scrub and sand. It was a diamond-shaped area at the bottom of the future state of of Nevada. Spanish explorers discovered the spot in 1829 and gave it the name Las Vegas, which means The Meadow. Captain John C. Fremont and his company camped here in 1843 but soon moved on. Later, the Mormons and a a few miners attempted to establish a settlement.

The real start of Las Vegas as an entity came in 1905. Railroad interests gave away parcels of land for five dollars each. These first plots of land are now the site of Casino Center, which covers an area of about five blocks, and the new multi-million-dollar Fremont Street Experience, a light show. Things were quiet from 1905 until 1931. Numerous saloons had begun to pop up, most of which had some form of gambling. There was also a red-light district, divided geographically into sections with "working girls" from various parts of the world. The houses with their "cribs" occupied the area now bounded by Main, Ogden, Stewart and Fourth streets, one block north of Fremont Street. It was shut down in 1941.

In the late 1920s, Hollywood became aware of this free-form, wide-open settlement in the middle of the

The legendary Sands Hotel

desert. A number of films were premiered here. Air-conditioning consisted of large fans blowing across cakes of ice and through wet towels into the theater. The premiere served as a good excuse for a Hollywood party away from home.

The year 1931 was an important one. Phil Tobin, Winnemucca rancher and Republican State assemblyman, was prevailed upon to introduce the enabling act that allowed legal gambling statewide. One story has it that he did so for two bottles of Scotch whiskey. Some even say that several Las Vegas Mormons provided the liquor. Did Mormons really provide Tobin with the whiskey? The question is moot. The important thing is that, with this law, Las Vegas and Nevada as we know it became possible. Another contributing factor: Legislation was passed at the same time that made it easier to get married and divorced—simpler and faster than anywhere else.

Just as important at the start of the 1930s was the construction of Hoover Dam (then Boulder Dam). Later in that decade, Nellis Gunnery Range was established, the forerunner of Nellis Air Force Base, which became an important base of operations during World War II and has since become a vital part of the Las Vegas economy. World War II and Nellis Air Force Base were also responsible for shutting down the prostitution business just north of Fremont Street. Prostitution has been illegal in Las Vegas and Clark County ever since, but it is legal in neighboring Nevada counties. Now it exists in Las Vegas illegally just as it does in every major city.

In the early 1930s, the Bingo Club (now the Sahara Hotel), the El Rancho, and Last Frontier (the first of three Frontier hotels on that site), were built as small, ranch-style operations. The Flamingo, further south, was the first luxury establishment on what was to become the Strip. It opened in the mid-1940s and featured Jimmy Durante and Xavier Cugat and his orchestra and was treated fictionally in the recent film *Bugsy.*

Wilbur Clark's Desert Inn kicked off the 1950s. Frank Sinatra made his Las Vegas debut.there in 1951. You could have dinner and a show for under ten dollars back then. (Very few hotels have dinner shows today. Prices for current top-production shows—Siegfried & Roy at the Mirage, "Mystere" next door at Treasure Island, or Michael Crawford's "EFX" at the MGM Grand—range from seventy

Blackjack at **MGM Grand**

to eighty-five dollars, drinks included, but not dinner). Then, in 1952, Danny Thomas opened the Sands. The hotel's Copa Room was to become the playground for Frank and the Rat Pack as they made films during the day, appeared twice a night in the showroom, and then took over the casino and lounge until the wee hours.

In the 1960s, Howard Hughes started buying out hotels, and the changeover from individual hotel ownership to corporate ownership had begun. This was good for me because, thanks to Walter Kane, the three main Hughes hotels—the Desert Inn, the Frontier, and the Sands—became my stomping grounds during the 1970s and 1980s.

Within the last decade, Kirk Kerkorian and Steve Wynn have again changed our city's direction with themed hotels. Kerkorian bought the Flamingo in the late 1960s and made it his training ground for the building of the International a few years later. He sold the Flamingo and the International to the Hilton chain in the 1970s, then built the first MGM Grand and sold that in turn to Bally's. Each of the Kerkorian hotels successively became the biggest in Las Vegas. The second MGM Grand, at the

northeast corner of Tropicana and the Strip, currently holds the title, with more than 5,000 rooms.

Steve Wynn began his Las Vegas life as manager of Southern Wine & Spirits. He bought stock in the Golden Nugget, eventually took it over, and made that hotel a Strip landmark in Casino Center, forcing the other hotels in that area to become competitive. His Mirage and Treasure Island are tremendously successful, and Bellagio, being built on the site of the Dunes Hotel, may become Las Vegas's most upscale establishment.

Add to these Bob Stupak's Stratosphere, which just opened and is sure to become an important tourist attraction as we approach the end of this century. The same should be true for the about-to-be-opened Monte Carlo, the New York, New York, and the just-approved Paris, France (to be located next door to Bally's on the Strip). The colossal ITT-Sheraton now owns the Desert Inn and Caesars Palace, and one can look for the giant hotel chain to become a strong contributor to Las Vegas's future economy.

Then there's Circus Circus, the brainchild of the late Jay Sarno, who was also responsible for the concept

behind Caesars Palace. Unlike Caesars Palace, Circus Circus was not a huge success—that is, until Reno's Bill Bennett & Co. took it over and things began to happen. The Circus Circus empire now includes Slots-a-Fun, Silver City, the Excalibur, the Luxor, and the Hacienda, plus a Circus Circus in Reno. The company also has a major interest in the Monte Carlo. The Hacienda is slated to be razed at the end of 1996 to make room for a three-resort, themed complex that will stretch more than a mile from the Luxor south to Russell Road.

As Las Vegas came of age, so did film and photography—with the perfection of color photography and other technical advances. The growth of the entertainment industry went hand in hand with the unprecedented growth of Las Vegas. A master of the art of photography, Santi Visalli shows a remarkable ability to capture the essence of this American city. It is an honor to be asked to contribute to Visalli's brilliant capturing of my home town—of the heart and pulse of the most exciting, fastest growing city in the world.

As Santi Visalli's pictures show, Las Vegas is more than Casino Center and the Strip. Las Vegas also includes the University of Nevada at Las Vegas, a major institution with an enrollment in excess of 20,000, one of the world's finest hotel schools, and cultural activities equal to those in much larger cities. Las Vegas has mountains, desert, and two of the world's greatest man-made wonders—Lake Mead and the Hoover Dam. With so many changes and so much building going on between now and the year 2000, the need to record the present-day city for posterity is greater than ever. I'm proud to be part of the effort. With several appearances already scheduled for this year at the MGM Grand Hollywood Theater, and more to come, I look forward to spending the rest of this century playing Las Vegas.

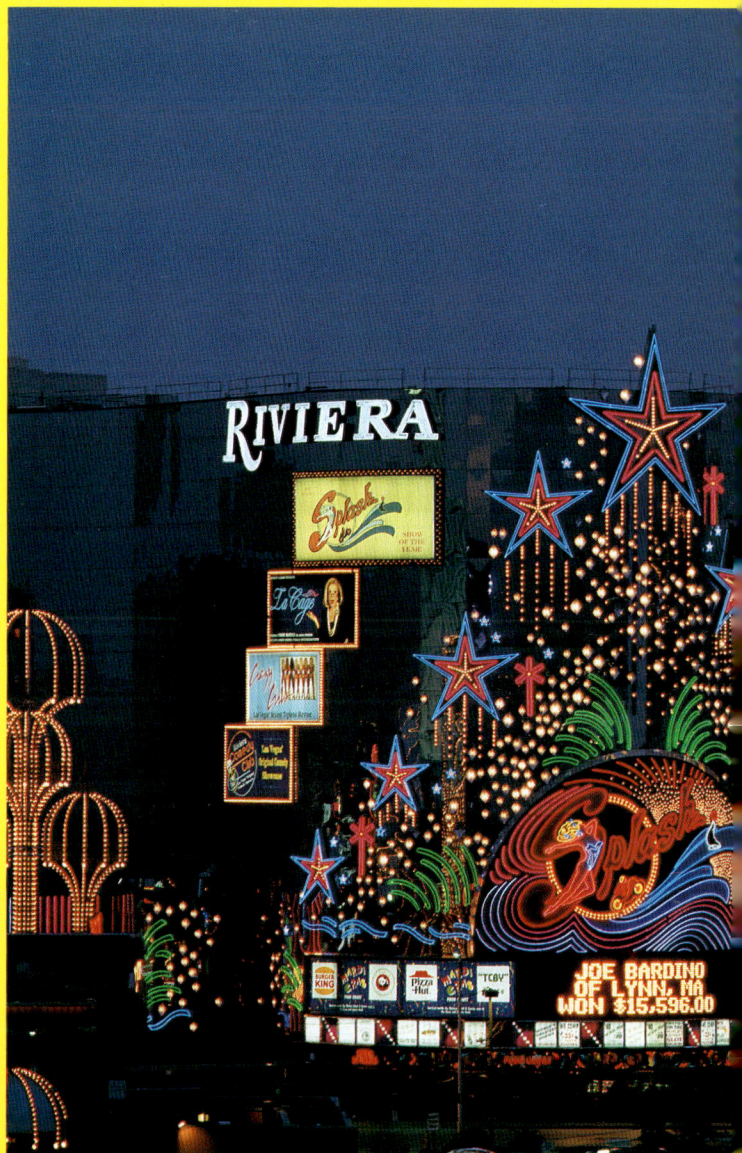

Left: Old slot machines at Gamblers General Store
Above: The Riviera Hotel and Casino

Gamblers General Store

Overleaf: Baccarat Room, MGM Grand

Above: Playing the slots. Right: Playing the slots, MGM Grand

Overleaf: Las Vegas license plates
Second overleaf: Billboards feed the gambling urge

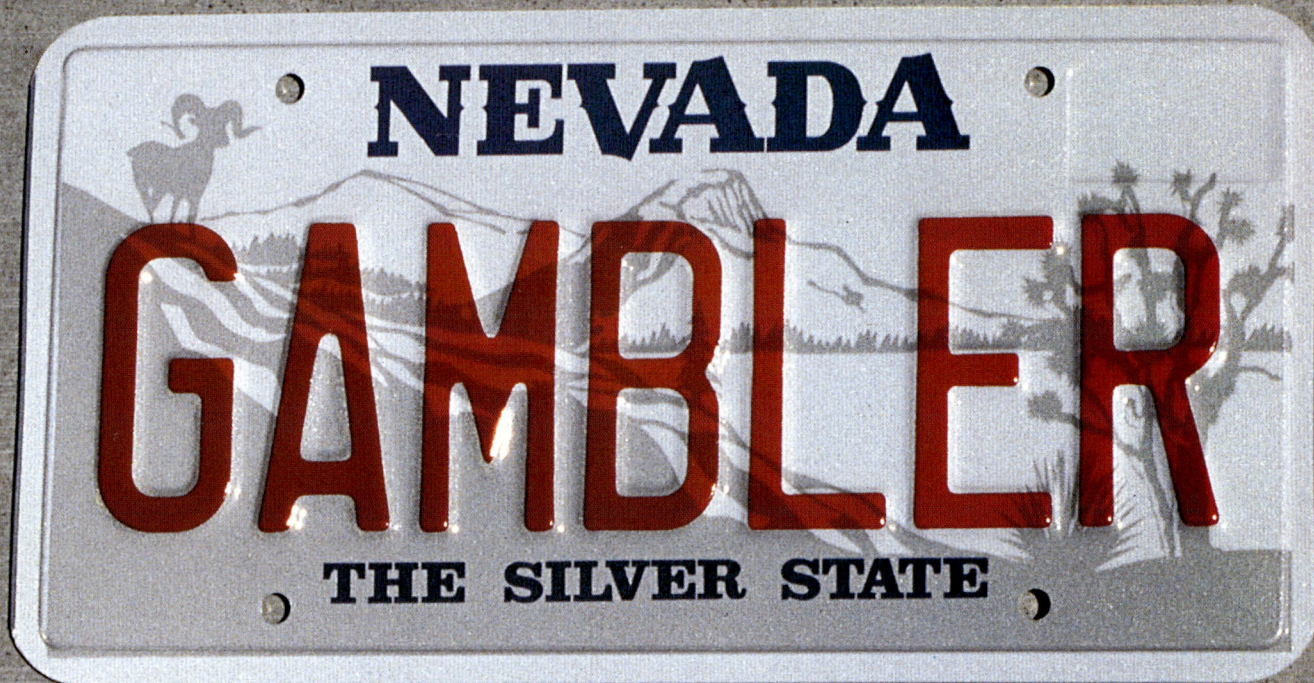

NEVADA
WINNER
THE SILVER STATE
NEVADA
LOSER
THE SILVER STATE

Billboard for Crazy Girls, *at the* Riviera Hotel

Newlyweds outside a drive-in wedding chapel

Candlelight Wedding Chapel, *one of the many places to be wed in Vegas*

Overleaf: Mike Tyson vs. Frank Bruno at the Garden Arena at MGM Grand

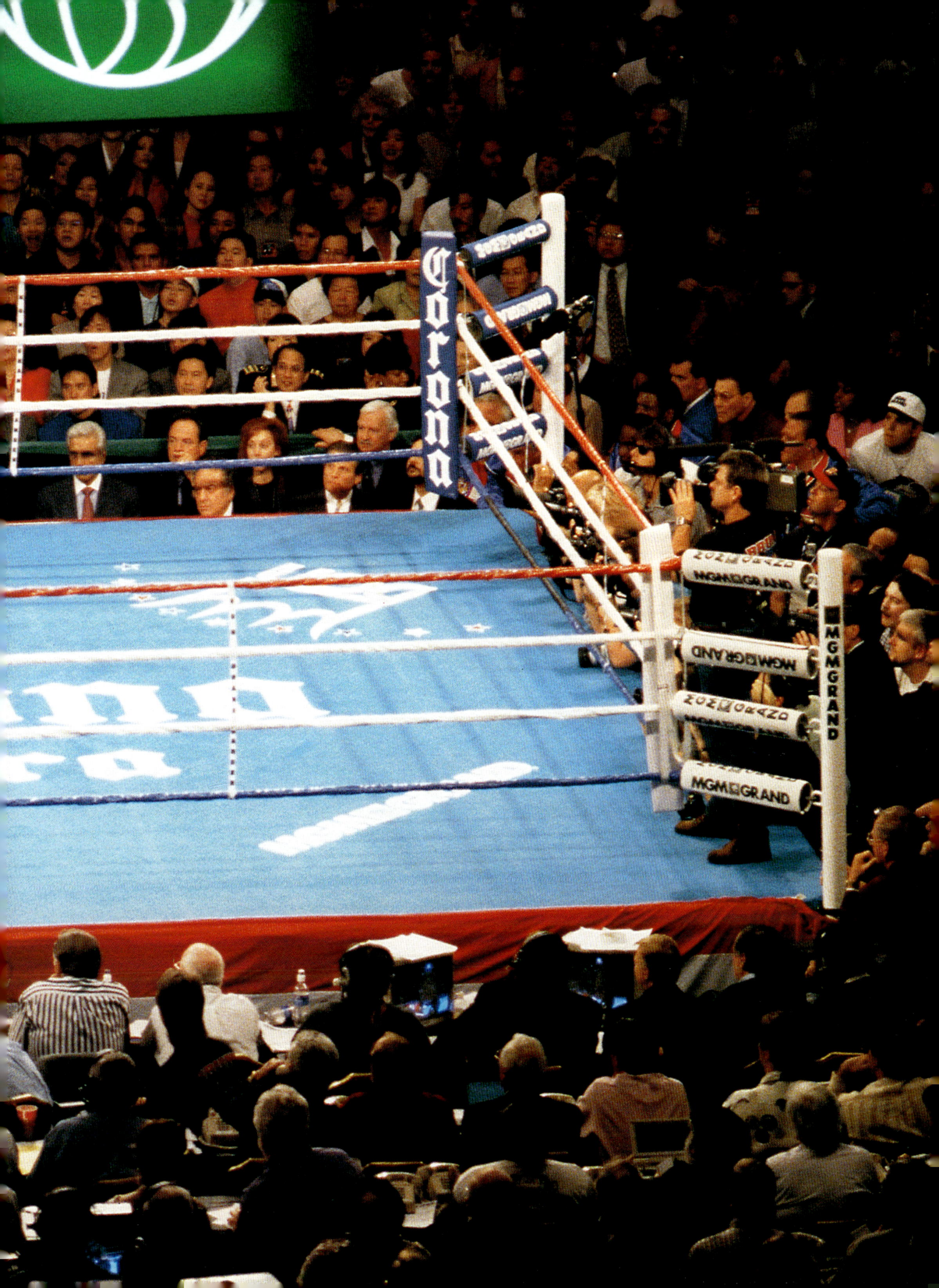

Mike Tyson vs. Frank Bruno at the **Garden Arena at MGM Grand**

Overleaf: Laser show at Sam's Town Hotel and Gambling Hall
Second overleaf: A scene from Spellbound, *a floorshow at* Harrah's

Above and right: Scenes from **Spellbound,** *a floorshow at* **Harrah's**

Overleaf: **Enter the Night,** *a floorshow at* **Stardust**

Enter the Night, *a floorshow at* Stardust

A ballet class at Fern Adair Conservatory of the Arts

Overleaf: Floorshow at Circus Circus

Liberace's bejewelled microphone on display at the Liberace Museum

Liberace's ornate cars in the Liberace Museum

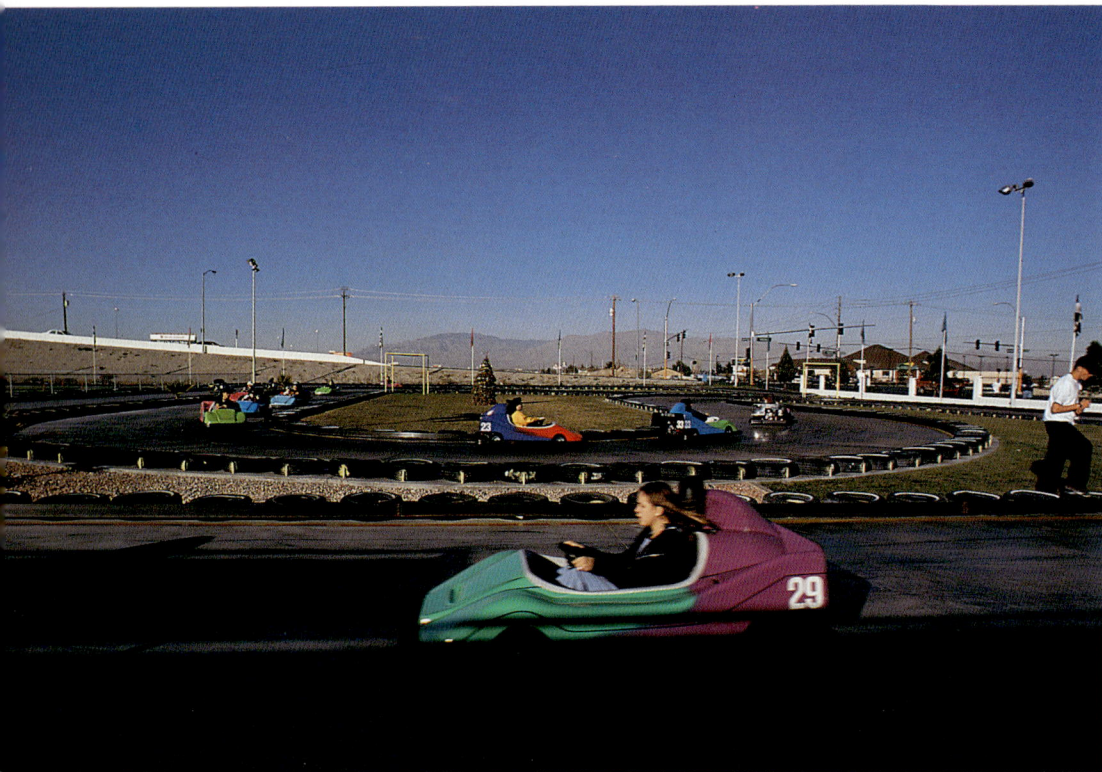

Mini Grand Prix *outside of Las Vegas*

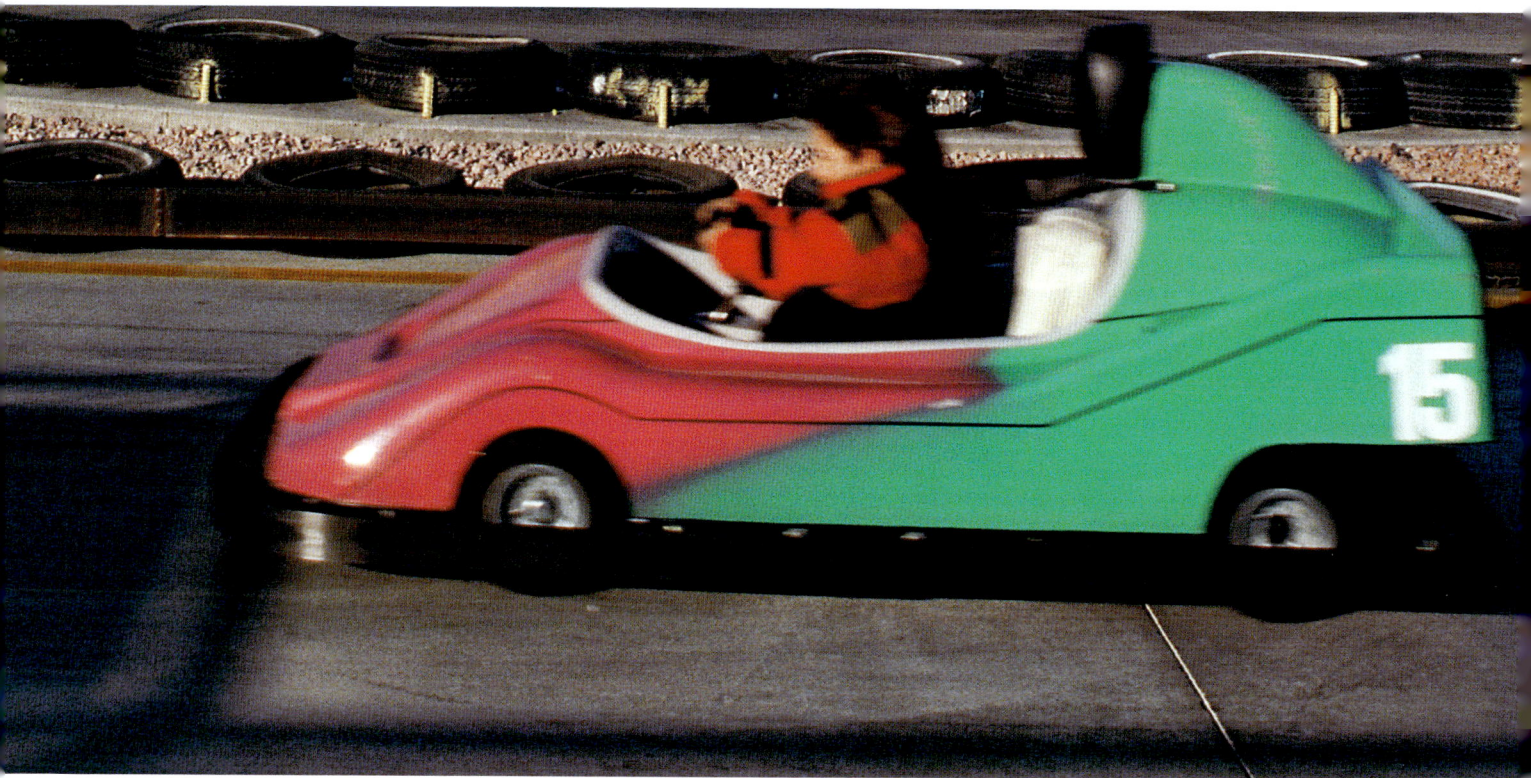

Overleaf: Recumbent cycler near **Bonnie Springs**

Bonnie Springs Ranch, *outside of Las Vegas*

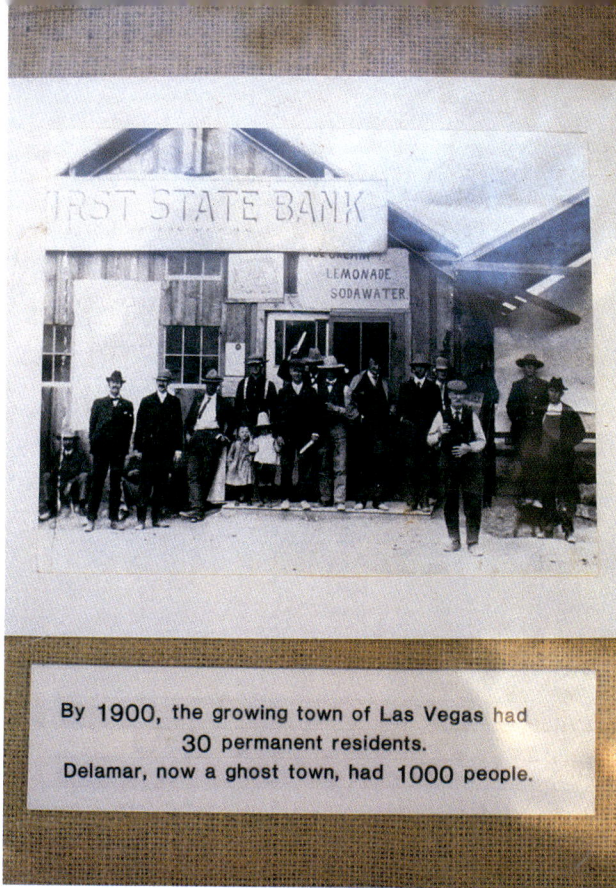

By 1900, the growing town of Las Vegas had
30 permanent residents.
Delamar, now a ghost town, had 1000 people.

Las Vegas, circa 1900

Lost City Museum, *Overton*

Overleaf: Bonnie Springs Ranch, *outside of Las Vegas*

Bonnie Springs Ranch, *outside of Las Vegas*

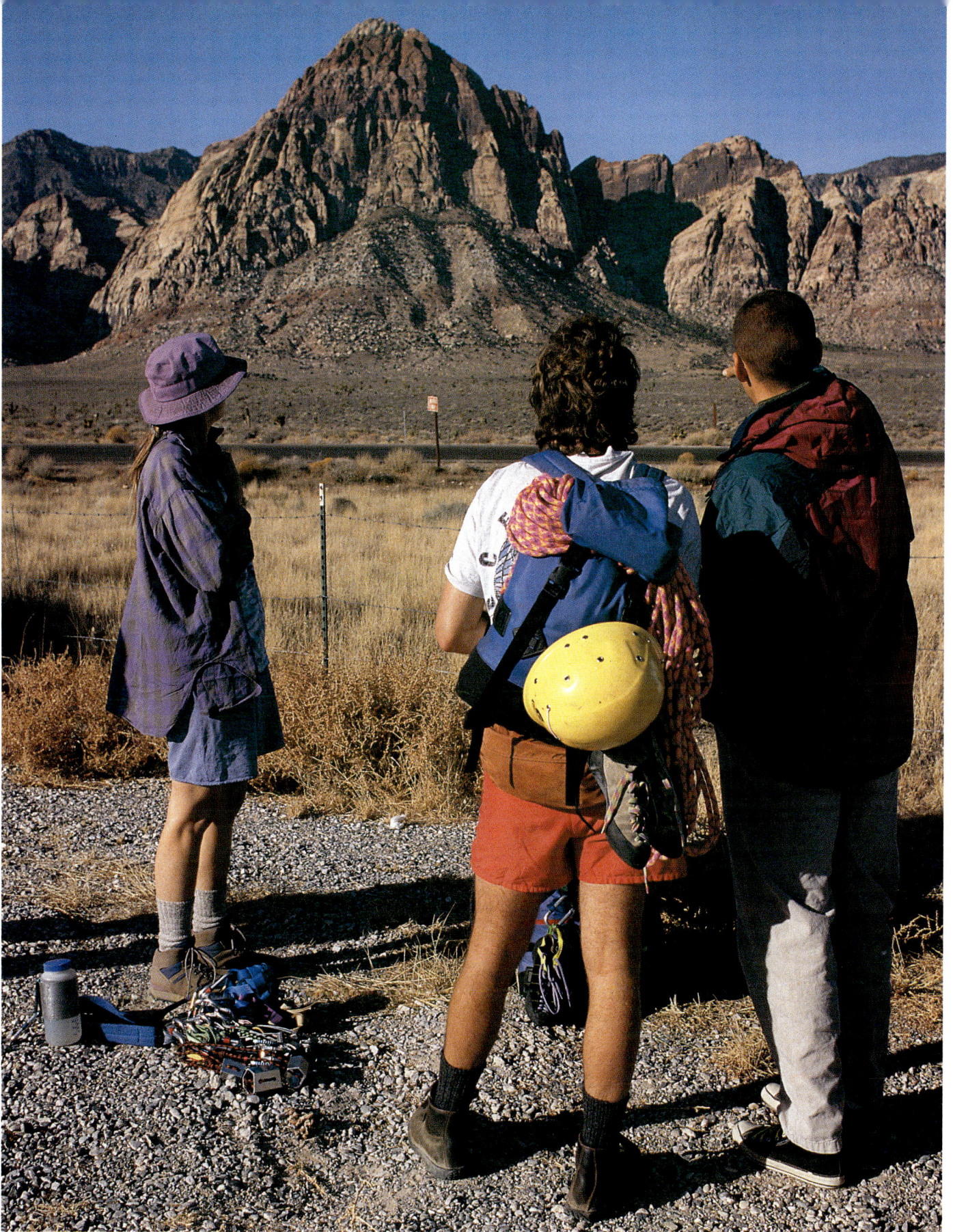

Rock climbers at Rainbow Mountain

Visitors Center, Red Rock Canyon

Overleaf: A Joshua tree in the desert near Overton
Second overleaf: A Joshua tree in Red Rock Canyon

Standing dead desert trumpet

Snakeweed and grasses of Red Rock Canyon

Rugged desert growth at Red Rock Canyon

Howard Hughes's Ranch, *outside of Las Vegas*

Luxor, *Las Vegas*

Overleaf: Desert trumpet at Red Rock Canyon;
Christmas Tree on Fremont Street

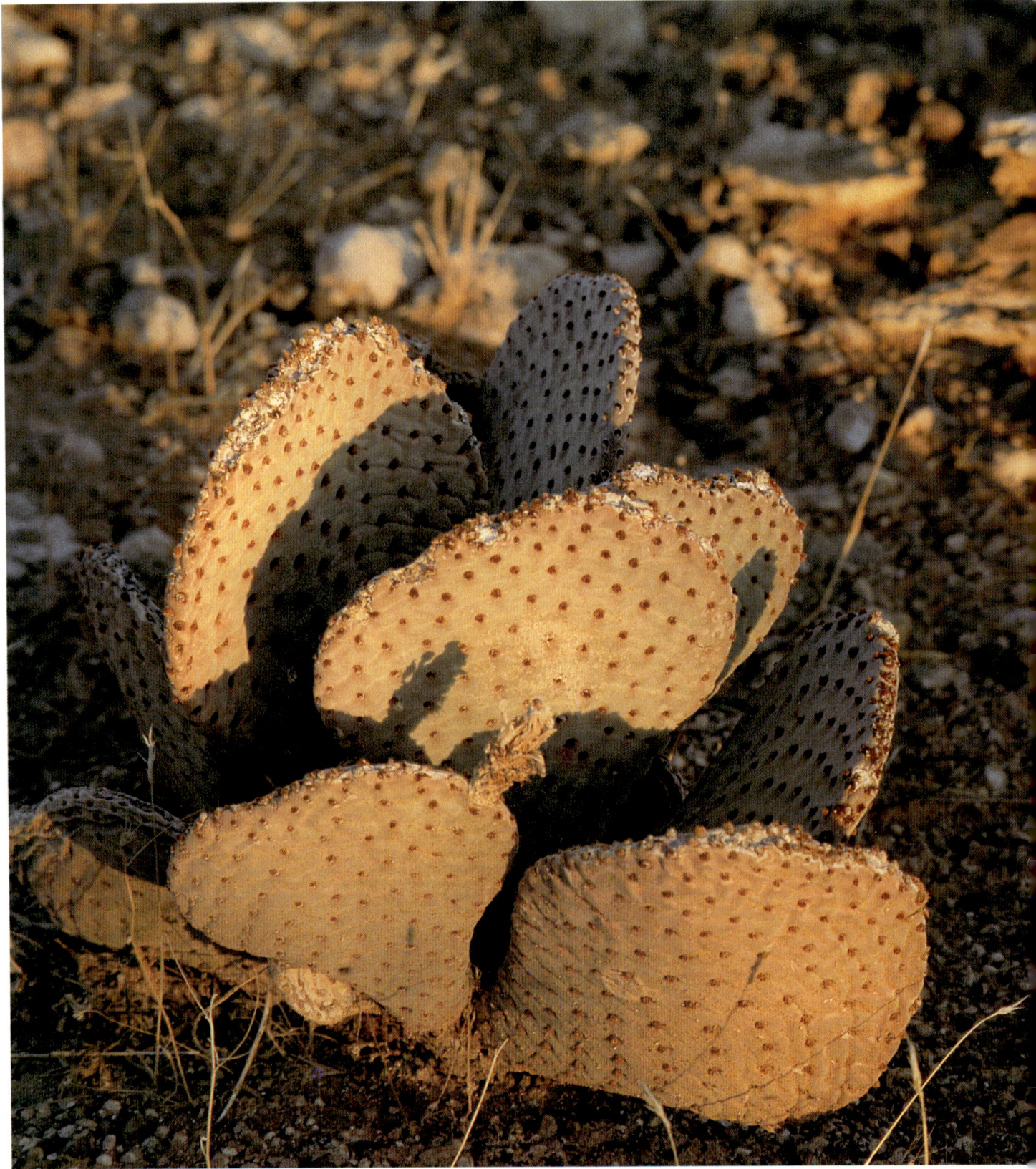

Above: Beavertail cactus in the Nevada desert. Right: **Cactus garden** *at Christmas*

Barrel cactus at Red Rock Canyon

Detail of the Flamingo Hilton

Detail of the Flamingo Hilton

Above: Harrah's Hotel and Casino

Left: Treasure Island

Overleaf: Bally's Hotel and Casino

Bally's Hotel and Casino

Roulette wheel at Harrah's

Playing the slots at Harrah's

Above and right: Blackjack table at **Harrah's**

Overleaf: MGM Grand Hotel and Theme Park
Second overleaf: **Luxor,** *Las Vegas*
Third overleaf: Caesars Palace

Las Vegas skyline

Above: Fountain in front of the Luxor. *Right : Special effect projection on the* Luxor Fountain

Real estate development outside of Las Vegas

The Luxor *and* McCarran International Airport

Nevada Landing Casino *on Highway 15*

Overleaf: View of Las Vegas from the Stratosphere *at twilight*

Second overleaf: Excalibur Hotel & Casino

EXCALIBUR

Gold Strike Inn *near the* Hoover Dam

The Thomas Mack Center *at the* University of Nevada

Overleaf: The Clark County Library, East Flamingo Street

Community College of Southern Nevada *in West Charleston*

Community College of Southern Nevada *in West Charleston*

University of Nevada *housing*

University of Nevada *housing*

Overleaf: The science building at UNLV
Second Overleaf: Facade of the restaurant Sfuzzi

Dive!, *a popular restaurant with an undersea theme*

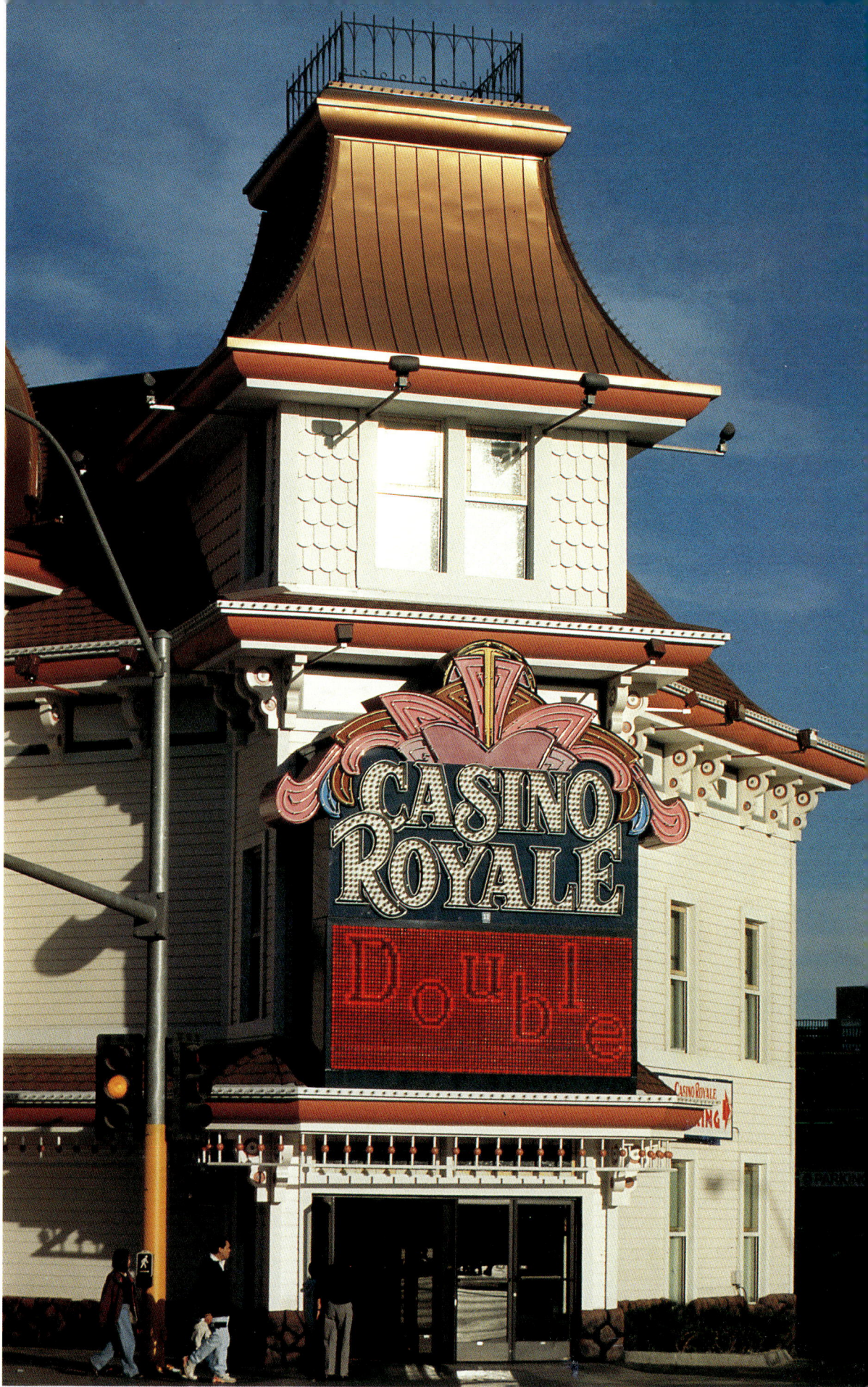

Casino Royale *on* the Strip

The dining room of Spago *in* Caesars Palace

Above : The Forum *at* Caesars Palace
Left: Treasure Island

Above: Retired neon sign at Young Electric Sign Co.

Left: Columns of the Aladdin Hotel

Overleaf: Retired neon sign at Young Electric Sign Co.

Second overleaf: Caesars Palace

Caesars Palace

Community College of Southern Nevada *in West Charleston*

Overleaf: The tallest building in the West, the **Stratosphere**

Above and right: Circus Circus

Overleaf: Grand Slam Canyon Theme Park, Circus Circus

EXIT

Fountains in front of **The Mirage**

Fruits of the Mojave yucca at **Red Rock Canyon**

Overleaf: **The Clark County Government Center**

Drink *nightclub*

Marina on Lake Mead

Oasis Golf Club *in Mesquite, Nevada*

Overleaf: Players Island Resort and Casino, *Mesquite*

Driving to Lake Mead

Oasis Golf Club *in Mesquite, Nevada*

Above and left: Golfers at the **Tournament Players Club,** *Summerlin*

Above: The Hoover Dam, *built in 1931. Right: Aerial view of the* Hoover Dam

Overleaf: The Hoover Dam

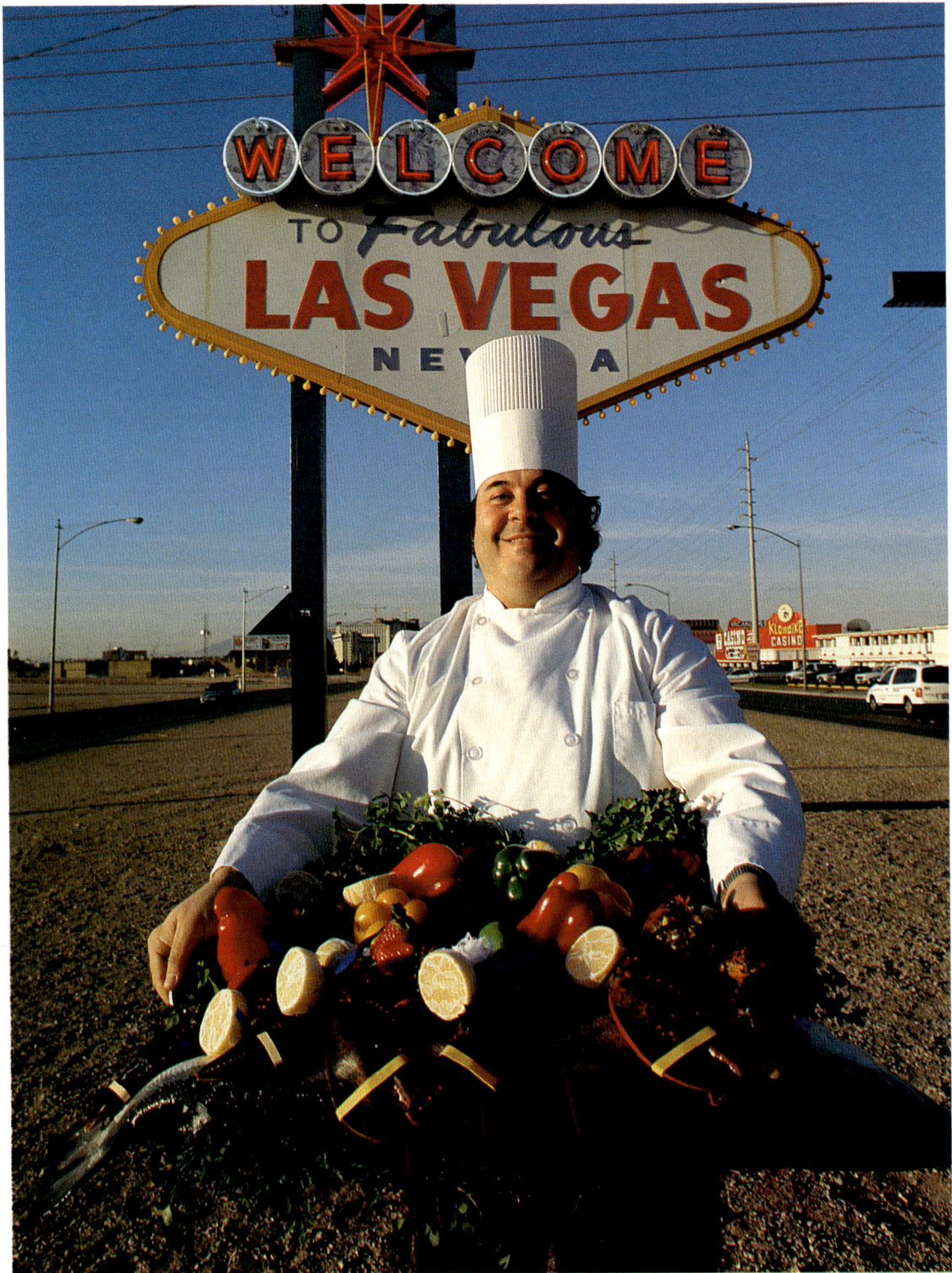

Above: Angelo Sanna, one of two chefs at the popular Las Vegas restaurant I Tre Visi. *Right: Doorman at* Treasure Island

Overleaf: Bins of chips at Gamblers General Store

The badge reads "Captain Black Front Services Doorman" and the blue button reads "Winter Vacations".

Lorenzo Lambert rolling cigars at **Don Pablo Cigar Co.**

Gambling theme neckties

Above: A poker chip lamp. Right: Gold telephones, MGM Grand

Above: Gun belonging to Sam Boyd, founder of Sam's Town Casino

Left: The world's largest gold nugget, at Golden Nugget

CHARLES "SONNY" L
1932 — 1970
'A MAN'

Sonny Liston's grave, Paradise Memorial Gardens

Redd Foxx's grave, Palm Valley View Memorial Cemetery

Overleaf: **The Hard Rock Cafe's** *famous logo, Las Vegas style*

Second overleaf: **The Strip** *at night*

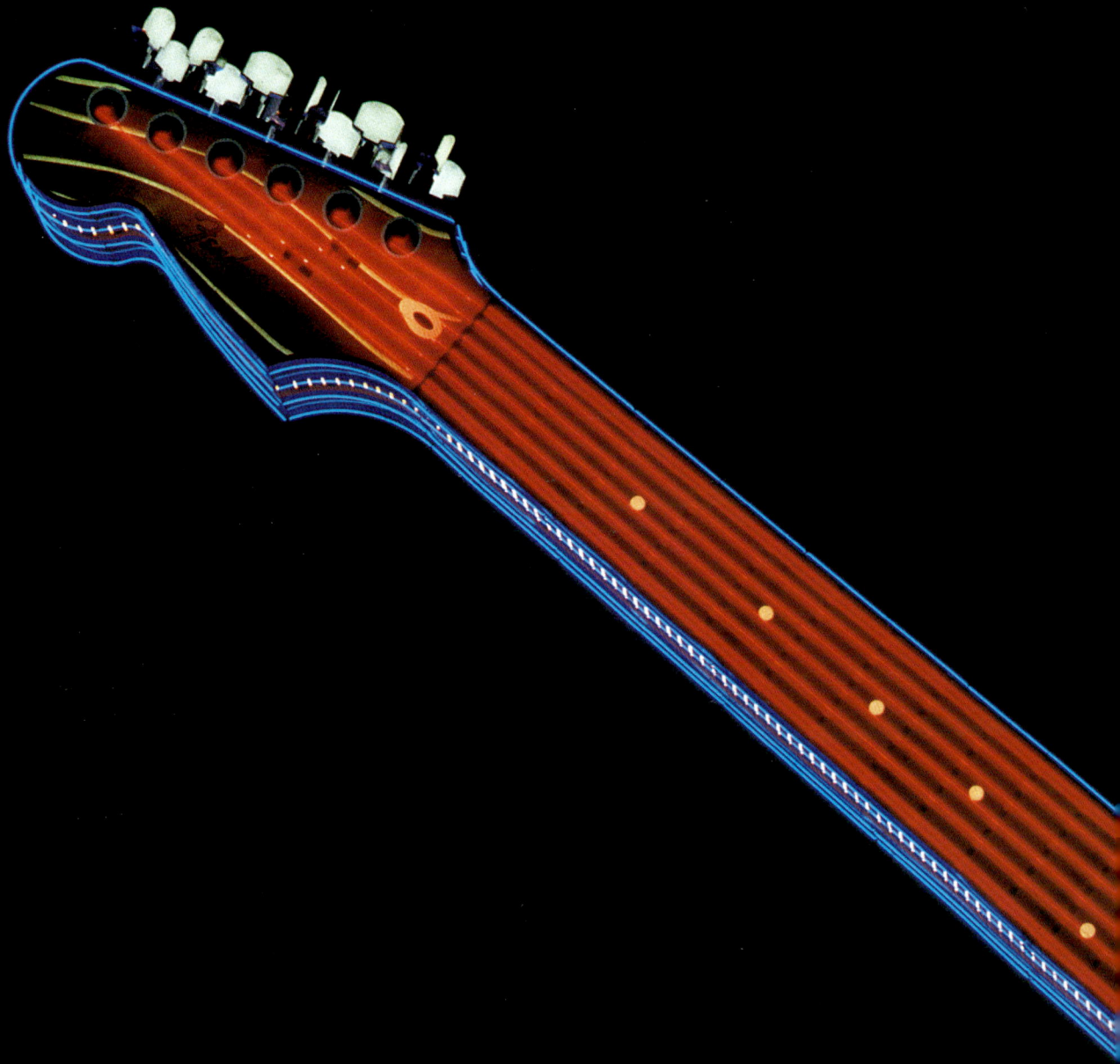

CASINO ROYALE

Denny's

Above: Patriot on **Fremont Street**

Left: Toy soldiers march on **Fremont Street**

Overleaf: Christmas in the **Flamingo's** *casino*

Second overleaf: **Wizard of Oz** *display at the* **MGM Grand;** **Excalibur** *at night*

The Strip *at night;* Barbary Coast *and the* Flamingo Hilton

Overleaf: Portion of Las Vegas skyline

Players Island Resort and Casino, *Mesquite*

Overleaf: *Nevada sunset*
Second overleaf: *Moon over Las Vegas*

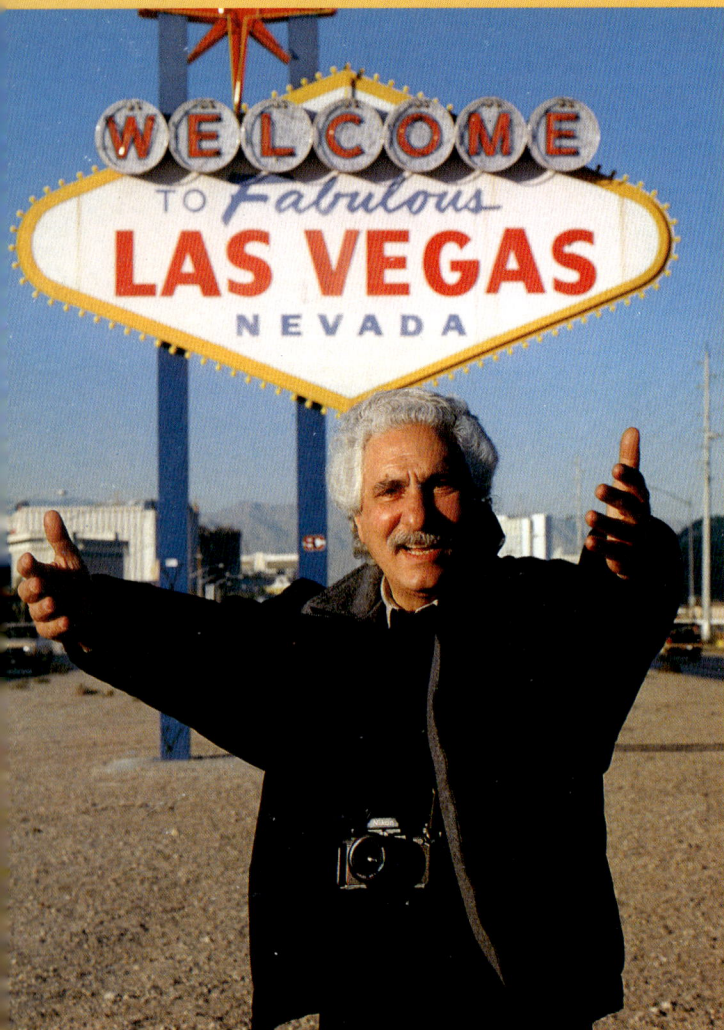

photo by Ivon Visalli

Santi Visalli

BIOGRAPHIES

Award-winning photojournalist Santi Visalli was born in Messina, Sicily, and has lived in the United States since 1959. His photographs have appeared in *Time, Newsweek,* and the *New York Times,* as well as in other leading newspapers and magazines throughout the world. Mr. Visalli is currently president of the Foreign Press Association of New York. In 1996, Santi Visalli was bestowed with the title of Knight in the Order of Merit of the Republic of Italy.

The consummate stage performer Wayne Newton has performed live to over 15 million people at last count. He most recently performed his 25,000th show on the Las Vegas Strip at the Sheraton Desert Inn, a landmark for any entertainer, and was named "Ambassador of Las Vegas" by the World Travel Association. His performances continue to sell out in Las Vegas, as well as at his own Wayne Newton Theater in Branson, Missouri, and around the world.

ACKNOWLEDGMENTS

A recent survey identified Las Vegas as the number one tourist destination in the US. Speaking from firsthand experience, I understand why the 90,000 rooms of the Las Vegas hotels and casinos are occupied year round. The entertainment capital of the world, Las Vegas is truly a "planet" of its own. Aside from such obvious pursuits as gambling, Las Vegas offers many other forms of entertainment for old and young alike. Going to Las Vegas today is like going to a big amusement park of the most sophisticated and high-tech quality. Like a mirage, Las Vegas evokes an inviting "island" in the desert.

Las Vegas is easy to photograph—everything has been done for you! It is like a big movie set where the best stage designers, directors, and choreographers have set everything up for you. You just aim and shoot and you have no surprises, but an interesting picture. However, obtaining the necessary permission to photograph is often another matter. Many shows, casinos, and amusement parks are off limits to professional photographers. Fortunately, through the intervention of Rob Powers, Public Relations Director of the Las Vegas Convention/Visitors Authority, I was able to do almost everything I set out to do. For this, I want to express my gratitude to him and to all the establishments appearing in this book.

I must also thank Kevin Deverich of the Griffin Group and Roy Young, General Manager of the Players Island Resort-Casino-Spa in Mesquite, for their generous hospitality and Sargent Chris Perry of the Nevada Highway Patrol. Additionally my appreciation goes to Pat Marvel and René Roberts of the Stratosphere for the use of their roof. Thanks to the army of valet parking attendants who, aware of the time pressure, brought my car in and out of the immense parking areas with speed of light.

Among the many other individuals to whom I am indebted are Dario Mariotti, Franco Nuschese, Michele Troiano, Ivon Visalli, and Melo Cicala for assisting me in one way or another in the production of this book. At Universe and Rizzoli, I extend sincere appreciation to Heather Keller, Charles Miers, James Stave, Elizabeth White, and to the many others for their contributions, together with my gratitude to the book's designers, Jenny Chan and Cynthia Flaxman. Finally, a very special salute and thank you to "Mr. Las Vegas" himself, Wayne Newton, for his foreword to this book.